Mission Furniture - Part III

1912

HENRY HAVEN WINDSOR

TABLE OF CONTENTS

NOTE   5

PART I. A PIANO BENCH   7

PART II. A FINISH   15

PART III. A WRITING DESK   21

PART IV. MAGAZINE RACK   29

PART V. A MISSION BOOKRACK   37

PART VI. ANOTHER PIANO BENCH   45

PART VII. A FOOT WARMER   53

NOTE

This book is one of the series of handbooks on industrial subjects being published by the Popular Mechanics Co. Like the magazine, these books are "written so you can understand it," and are intended to furnish information on mechanical subjects at a price within the reach of all.

The texts and illustrations have been prepared expressly for this Handbook Series, by experts; are up-to-date, and have been revised by the editor of Popular Mechanics.

The dimensions given in the stock list contained in the description of each piece of furniture illustrated in this book call for material mill-planed, sanded and cut to length. If the workman desires to have a complete home-made article, allowance must be made in the dimensions for planing and squaring the pieces. S-4-S and S-2-S are abbreviations for surface four sides and surface two sides.

PART I. A PIANO BENCH

A PIANO BENCH

The piano bench shown in the accompanying picture was made of black walnut and was finished natural. The finish was applied in the following manner: First, all the parts were well scraped and sandpapered, then the surface was covered with a coating of boiled linseed oil. After this had stood several hours, or until it had had time to penetrate the wood, the surplus liquid was wiped off with a flannel cloth. After the oil had stood for 48 hours, a thin coat of shellac was applied and allowed to harden overnight. The next morning this shellac was sandpapered lightly with No. 00 paper and a coat of floor wax was applied according to the directions which are found upon every can. Two more coats of wax were applied after intervals of half an hour and the finish was completed. The effect is very pleasing. The oil brings out the rich color of the wood and the shellac and wax serve to preserve the color. The following stock is needed:

1 top, 1 by 16-1/2 by 40-1/2 in., S-2-S.
4 posts, 1-1/2 by 1-1/2 by 20 in., S-4-S.
2 rails, 7/8 by 4-1/4 by 36 in., S-2-S.
2 rails, 7/8 by 4-1/4 by 13 in., S-2-S.
2 lower rails, 7/8 by 2-1/2 by 13 in., S-2-S.
1 stretcher, 7/8 by 3-3/4 by 36 in., S-2-S.
6 slats, 3/8 by 1-1/4 by 11 in., S-2-S.

With the exception of the legs all the stock is specified mill-planed to thickness upon two surfaces. The legs are specified planed on four sides. Square the legs to length and the rails, stretcher, slats, etc., to width and length.

Lay out and work the tenons of the rails and stretcher. The slats are best made without tenons, the whole end of each slat being "housed" into the rails. The reason for this is obvious—it is a difficult matter to fit two or more pieces between fixed parts when their ends are tenoned. When the ends are housed any slight variation in the lengths adjusts itself. It is necessary, however, to chisel the sides of the mortises carefully, but this is a simple matter compared with getting the shoulders of the tenons, etc., all just alike.

Assemble the parts, using good hot glue. Put the ends of the bench together first. When the glue has hardened on these, place the stretcher and side rails. Fasten the top to the frame from the under side, either by glued blocks and screws or by angle irons.

A LIBRARY TABLE

A library table of neat appearance and correct proportions is shown in the accompanying sketch and detail drawing. This table looks best when finished in quarter-sawed oak, although any of the other furniture woods can be used if desired. If the material is ordered from the mill cut to length, squared and sanded, much of the hard labor can be avoided. Order the following pieces:

4 legs, 2 by 2 by 30-1/4 in., S-4-S.
1 top, 1-1/8 by 30 by 42 in., S-4-S.
2 end pieces, 3/4 by 17-1/8 by 29 in., S-2-S.
2 top rails, 7/8 by 2 by 37 in., S-4-S.
2 top rails, 7/8 by 2 by 25-1/2 in., S-4-S.
1 lower brace, 3/4 by 2 by 32 in., S-4-S.
4 shelves, 3/4 by 7 by 29 in., S-4-S.
8 slats, 1/4 by 1-1/8 by 17-1/8 in., S-4-S.
2 drawer fronts, 3/4 by 5-3/4 by 25 in., S-4-S.
4 drawer sides, 3/8 by 3-3/4 by 14 in., soft wood.
2 drawer ends, 3/8 by 3-3/8 by 24-1/4 in., soft wood.
2 drawer bottoms, 3/8 by 13-1/4 by 24-1/4 in., soft wood.
2 drawer supports, 3/4 by 2 by 23-1/2 in., soft wood.
2 drawer supports, 3/4 by 2 by 25 in., soft wood.

Start work on the legs by beveling the tops and squaring them up and laying out the mortises for the shelves as shown in section BB. Care should be taken to get the legs mortised in pairs and all cut the same height. This is best done by placing the four legs side by side with the ends square, and then laying out the mortises across all four at once with a try-square.

The table top is made of several boards which are doweled and glued together. Be careful to get the best side of each board up and have the joints a tight fit. The corners should be cut out for the posts as shown. The posts are to be fastened to the board by means of screws. The holes can be counterbored for the heads and then plugged. The top rails are also fastened to the top board by means of screws.

The end pieces can now be made. Two or more boards will have to be glued together for these. The top corners will have to be cut to fit about the top rails. Cleats can be used in fastening them to the top board. The shelves also have the corners cut to fit into the mortises in the posts. They are held to the end boards by means of screws.

If the parts all fit perfectly square and tight, they can be glued and screwed together, which will complete the table except for the slats and drawers. The slats can be fastened on with nails, then the heads covered with fancy nails which can be secured for this purpose. The drawer supports can now be put in. They are screwed to the end boards as shown. A bottom brace should be fastened under the lower shelves to help steady the table. The two drawers are made as shown in the detail sketch. No handles are needed as the lower edge of the front board can be used for pulling them out.

When the table is complete it should be carefully gone over with fine sandpaper and all rough spots removed. Scrape the glue from about the joints as finish will not take where there is any glue. Apply the stain preferred or the one that matches the other furniture. This can be any of the many stains supplied by the trade for this purpose.

A PRINCESS DRESSER

A design of a princess dresser that is well proportioned and of pleasing appearance is shown in the accompanying sketch and detail drawing. The cost is very moderate and if a mill is not too far away, a great amount of labor can be saved by ordering the material ready cut to length, squared and sanded. Quarter-sawed oak should be used and the material needed will be as follows:

4 posts, 1-3/4 by 1-3/4 by 27 in., S-4-S.
1 top board, 3/4 by 17 by 37 in., S-2-S.
5 side rails, 3/4 by 1-1/2 by 37-1/2 in., S-4-S.
4 end rails, 3/4 by 2 by 17-1/2 in., S-4-S.
2 end panels, 1/4 by 16-1/4 by 16-3/4 in., S-4-S.
1 drawer partition, 1 by 7-3/4 by 18-1/2 in., S-4-S.
1 back board, 3/4 by 4-1/2 by 36 in., S-2-S.
2 mirror supports, 7/8 by 2-1/2 by 30 in., S-4-S.
2 side pieces for mirror, 3/4 by 2 by 42 in., S-4-S.
2 end pieces for mirror, 3/4 by 2 by 21-1/2 in., S-4-S.
2 drawer fronts, 3/4 by 7 by 17-1/2 in., S-4-S.
1 drawer front, 3/4 by 7 by 36 in., S-4-S.
1 20 by 38 bevel mirror.

The following pieces may be of any soft wood:
5 drawer slides, 3/4 by 2 by 17 in.
6 drawer sides, 1/2 by 7 by 17 in.
2 drawer bottoms, 1/2 by 17 by 17 in.
1 drawer bottom, 1/2 by 17 by 35-1/2 in.
4-1/2 sq. ft. of 3/8-in. pine for back.

First be sure the posts are perfectly square and of equal length. Either chamfer or round the upper ends as desired. The mortises can now be laid out and cut or they can be left until the rail tenons are all made and then marked and cut directly from each tenon. The posts as well as the end rails should have grooves cut in them to take the 1/4-in. end panels.

The top board should have the corners cut to fit about the posts. The corners of the back board should be rounded as shown in the drawing.

The end sections of the dresser can be glued together first, care being taken to get the joints square and tight. When these are dry the side rails and drawer slides can be fitted and glued in place. The top board is held in position by means of screws through cleats which are fastened to the inner sides of the rails.

The mirror frame is made by mortising the end pieces with the side pieces as shown. It is rabbeted on the back to hold a 20 by 38-in. mirror. After the mirror is securely fastened in the frame a thin wood covering should be tacked on the back to protect the glass. The frame swings between two upright posts which are securely fastened to the body of the dresser as shown.

The drawers are made and fitted in the usual manner. The drawing shows two drawers in the top compartment, but one exactly like the lower can be made and used instead by simply leaving out the 1 in. partition. Suitable handles for the drawers can be purchased at any hardware store.

The back is made of soft wood and is put on in the usual manner. Scrape all surplus glue from about the joints as the stain will not take where there is any glue. Finish smooth with fine sandpaper and apply the stain desired, which may be any of the many mission stains supplied by the trade for this purpose.

A SEWING BOX

A rather unique sewing box, and one that is quite as convenient as unique, is shown in the illustration. The material is walnut and ash. The posts are walnut and the slats and top rail ash. Both are finished in their natural colors. The following is the stock bill:
4 posts, 1-1/2 in. in diameter and 15 in. long, walnut.
1 bottom, 3/8 by 16-1/2 by 16-1/2 in., S-2-S, walnut.
4 top rails, 3/8 by 1-1/2 by 20 in., S-2-S, ash.

4 under rails, 5/8 by 3/4 by 20 in., S-2-S, walnut.

72 slats, 1/8 by 5/8 by 6-1/2 in., S-2-S, ash.

In ordering the stock it will be wise to combine the lengths of pieces having like widths and thicknesses.

If not possible to secure doweling of the diameter indicated for the verticals, it is an easy matter to take a square piece of stock, lay it off and work it into an eight-sided prism. After this, the arrises may again be planed until it has 16 and then 32 sides. The rest may be removed with sandpaper. Or it is possible that curtain pole stock will be available. Saw these posts to length and leave the ends square.

Square up the stock for the other parts. Work the bottom piece to a 16-in. square. The rails are not to be squared on the ends but are to be mitered each in turn. The bottom is fastened to the posts by metal brackets.

Chisel out recesses in the posts so that the bottom may be inserted. Insert the corners and use glue and nails to hold them in place. Place the lower of the two top rails, notching out the posts as is necessary to bring the inner edge of these rails in position. Fasten to the posts. Miter and place the top rails. The slats, it will be noted, are fastened to the bottom from the outer side and to the lower of the two top rails from the inner side. Brass-headed tacks such as upholsterers use are required.

In finishing, sandpaper all parts and then apply a coat of boiled linseed oil. Allow this to stand a half hour or so and then wipe the surface clean. After this has dried thoroughly apply a thin coating of shellac and allow it to harden. Sand the shellac when hard with No. 00 sandpaper and then apply several coats of wax, polishing in the usual manner.

Two pairs of castors will add to the ease with which the box may be moved about.

A FERN STAND

When making the fern stand shown in the accompanying sketch use quarter-sawed oak if possible, as this wood is the most suitable for finishing in the different mission stains. Considerable labor can be saved in its construction by ordering the stock from the mill ready cut to length, squared and sanded. Order the following pieces:

4 posts, 1-1/2 by 1-1/2 by 30 in., S-4-S.

8 side rails, 3/4 by 1-1/2 by 13-1/2 in., S-4-S.

2 shelf supports, 3/4 by 1 by 13-1/2 in., S-4-S.

1 top, 3/4 by 16 by 16 in., S-4-S.

1 shelf, 3/4 by 15 by 15 in., S-4-S.

16 slats, 3/8 by 3 by 5 in., S-4-S.

The legs are made first. Be sure they are square and of equal length. The mortises can be laid out and cut or they can be left until the tenons on the side rails are all made, then marked and cut from each tenon. The top rails and the slats are exactly alike for the four sides, as the table is square. In addition to the tenons on the rails, grooves should be cut in each for the ends of the slats to fit into as shown in the cross section in the detail drawing. Holes should be cut in the slats as shown.

The top board should have the corners cut out to fit around the posts. It is held in place by means of screws through cleats which are fastened to the inner sides of the top rails.

The bottom board or shelf rests upon two rails that are mortised into the posts as shown. The top and bottom boards should be of one piece if possible, otherwise two or more boards will have to be glued together.

Before gluing up the joints see that all the pieces fit together square and tight. The posts and rails should be glued and assembled, then the top and bottom boards put in place to hold the frame square when the clamps are put on.

Leave to dry for about 24 hours before removing the clamps. Fasten the top and bottom boards in place and then go over the stand with fine sandpaper and remove all surplus glue and rough spots.

A WARDROBE

The wardrobe or clothes closet shown in the accompanying sketch and detail drawing will be found a great convenience in a bedroom where closet space is limited or where there is no closet at all. It provides ample room for hanging suits, dresses and other wearing apparel, as well as space for boots and shoes. It can be made of any of the several furniture woods in common use, but quarter-sawed oak will be found to give the most pleasing effect. The stock should be ordered from the mill ready cut to length, squared and sanded. In this way much labor will be saved. The following pieces will be needed:

4 posts, 1-3/4 by 1-3/4 by 64-1/2 in., S-4-S.
2 front rails, 3/4 by 1-1/2 by 37-1/2 in., S-4-S.
1 top and 1 bottom board, each 3/4 by 18-1/2 by 37 in., S-4-S.
1 top back rail, 3/4 by 4-1/4 by 37-1/2 in., S-4-S.
1 lower back rail, 3/4 by 4 by 37-1/2 in., S-4-S.
6 end rails, 3/4 by 6 by 18-1/2 in., S-4-S.
4 end uprights, 3/4 by 4 by 22-1/2 in., S-4-S.
8 end panels, 3/8 by 7-1/2 by 22-1/2 in., S-4-S.
5 shelves, 3/4 by 17-3/4 by 19-1/2 in., S-4-S.
2 drawer fronts, 3/4 by 4-3/4 by 8-1/2 in., S-4-S.
1 door, 3/4 by 7-3/4 by 10 in., S-4-S.
1 shelf partition, 3/4 by 10 by 19 in., S-4-S.
2 drawer fronts, 3/4 by 7 by 17 in., S-4-S.

1 drawer front, 3/4 by 8 by 17 in., S-4-S.

1 partition (several pieces), 3/4 by 19-1/2 by 57-3/4 in., S-4-S.

4 door uprights, 3/4 by 2-1/2 by 57 in., S-4-S.

2 top rails, 3/4 by 3-1/2 by 14-1/2 in., S-4-S.

2 middle rails, 3/4 by 6 by 14-1/2 in., S-4-S.

2 lower rails, 3/4 by 4-1/2 by 14-1/2 in., S-4-S.

4 center uprights, 3/4 by 2-1/2 by 23 in., S-4-S.

8 panels, 3/8 by 6 by 22-1/2 in., S-4-S.

4 pieces, 3/8 by 4-3/4 by 19 in., soft wood.

2 pieces, 3/8 by 8 by 19 in., soft wood.

2 pieces, 3/8 by 4-1/4 by 8 in., soft wood.

4 pieces, 1/2 by 7 by 19 in., soft wood.

3 pieces, 1/2 by 16-1/2 by 19 in., soft wood.

2 pieces, 1/2 by 6-1/2 by 16-1/2 in., soft wood.

2 pieces, 1/2 by 8 by 19 in., soft wood.

1 piece, 1/2 by 7-1/2 by 16-1/2 in., soft wood.

1 back (several pieces), 3/8 by 36 by 58 in., S-2-S.

First be sure the posts are perfectly square and of equal length. The upper ends can be chamfered or rounded if desired. The two front posts are alike, as are the back ones. The mortises should be laid out in each pair of posts and then cut with a sharp chisel, or they can be left until the tenons are all made, and then marked and cut from each tenon. Grooves should be cut on one side of all the posts to take the end panels.

The front and lower back rails are plain except for the tenons at each end, but the end rails and the center uprights should have grooves cut for the panels the same as the posts. The top back rail serves as a top back board and should have the corners rounded as shown in the detail drawing.

The frame can now be assembled. Glue should be used on all the joints as it makes them much stiffer. Be careful to get the frame together perfectly square, or it will be hard to fit the doors and the shelves.

The top and bottom boards should have the corners cut to clear the posts. The closet is divided into two compartments by a partition. This can be made of plain boards or panels similar to those in the ends, as desired. Place the shelves in position as shown. They are held in place by means of cleats and screws. The one shelf has a partition in its center with a door on one side and two small drawers on the other. Drawers should be fitted to three of the other compartments. They are made in the usual manner except that the front boards should be cut out at the top for a handhold as shown.

The doors are fitted by a tenon and mortise joint at the ends. They have a centerpiece and panels to match the ends of the closet. Suitable hinges and a catch should be supplied. These can be purchased at any hardware store.

The backing is put on in the usual manner. It should be finished on the front side.

When complete, the closet should be carefully gone over with fine sandpaper and all glue and rough spots removed. Apply stain of the desired color. This may be any of the many mission stains supplied by the trade for this purpose.

PART II. A FINISH

A FINISH

An appropriate finish is obtained as follows: First thoroughly scrape and sandpaper the various parts, then apply a coat of brown Flemish water stain. Allow this to dry well, then sand it lightly with No. 00 sandpaper to lay the grain. Again apply the Flemish stain, but this time have it weakened by the addition of an equal amount of water. When dry, sand again as on the first coat. Upon the second coat of stain apply a thin coat of shellac. This is to protect the high lights from the stain in the filler which is to follow. Sand lightly, then apply a paste filler of a sufficiently dark shade to make a dark field for the brown Flemish. Clean off the surplus and polish in the usual manner.

Upon the filler, after it has hardened overnight, apply a coat of orange shellac. Successively apply several coats of some good rubbing varnish. Polish the first coats with haircloth or curled hair, and the last with pulverized pumice stone, mixed with raw linseed or crude oil.

AN OAK TABLE

The accompanying illustration shows another style of a mission table. The stock for this table if ordered as follows and sanded will require only the work of making the joints and putting them together:

4 posts, 2 in, square 30-5/8 in., S-4-S.
4 upper rails, 7/8 by 6-1/2 by 22-1/2 in., S-2-S.
2 lower rails, 7/8 by 3 by 22-1/2 in., S-2-S.
2 top pieces, 7/8 by 12-1/2 by 24-1/2 in., S-2-S.
6 slats, 3/8 by 3-1/2 by 15-1/2 in., S-2-S.
1 stretcher, 7/8 by 8-1/2 by 21-1/2 in., S-2-S.

This table may be made with mortise and tenon joints or with dowels as desired. If dowels are used, the upper and lower rails should be made 2 in. shorter than shown in the drawing.

Be sure to get the pieces for the posts with their surfaces square to each other and their ends sawed square off. This will simplify the assembling a great deal. Make the posts exactly the same length, 30-1/2 in., and chamfer a 3/8-in, bevel on their tops.

Square up the four upper rails, 6 by 22 in., marking the working face and edge to work from when laying out the tenons later. Square up the two lower rails, 2-1/2 by 22 in. These must be exactly the same length as the upper rails. The two ends of the table having the slats should be glued up first. Lay out the tenons on the upper and lower rails for these two ends and be sure to work from the marked face and edges, using a knife line. Cut the tenons, and, by placing them against the posts in the exact position they are to occupy, mark the places for the mortises. These joints should be numbered so that each mortise may be cut to fit its own tenon.

Square up the slats, 3 by 15-1/8 in., and cut mortises in the upper and lower rails 1/4 in. deep to let them in. The number of these slats, their size and spacing may be arranged to suit one's own idea. Put the posts, upper and lower rails, and slats together without glue first to determine if the parts fit properly, and then glue and clamp them together. Hot glue will hold best, if the room and lumber are warm; if not, it is best to use ordinary liquid glue. While the glue on these two ends of the table is setting, the other upper rails, top, and stretcher may be finished.

The top will have to be made of two or three pieces joined together with dowels and glue. If possible, use only two boards and be sure the grain in both pieces runs the same way when they are put together.

After the ends which were glued have set at least 24 hours, the clamps may be taken off and the other two upper rails tenoned and mortised in place. The stretcher may be held with two 3/8-in. dowels in each end, or with two round-head screws put through the lower rails. When gluing up the whole table, be sure the sides are square to each other. The top may now be squared up 24 by 24 in. and the corners cut out for the top of the posts. The top may be fastened as shown at A and B in the drawing, or by cleats screwed to the inside of the upper rails and top.

Before staining, be sure that all surplus glue is scraped off and the surfaces sanded clean. A weathered or fumed oak stain is suitable for this table. A good weathered oak stain may be made by mixing a little drop black ground in oil with turpentine and a little linseed oil. Put this stain on with a brush and allow to stand until it begins to flatten or dull, then rub off across the grain with a rag or piece of cotton waste. When thoroughly dry, apply one coat of very thin shellac. After this has dried, finish with two coats of wax. The shellac prevents the turpentine in the wax from rubbing out the stain. To get a good wax finish the work should dry until it will not show finger marks, before rubbing.

BOOK TROUGH

A very cheap but attractive book trough is shown in the accompanying photograph. This piece of mission furniture will be found useful in the home or office and can be made by anyone who has a slight knowledge of tools. The material should be either oak or chestnut, which can be secured from the planing mill dressed and sandpapered ready to cut the tenons and mortises. The stock needed will be as follows:

2 ends, 7/8 in. by 10 in. by 31 in., S-2-S.
1 shelf, 7/8 in. by 10 in. by 35 in., S-1-S.
2 trough pieces, 7/8 in. by 4 in. by 35 in., S-2-S.
8 keys, 5/8 in. by 5/8 in. by 3 in.

The two end pieces should be made first with the top corners rounded off and the lower end, which is of simple design, can be cut out with a bracket saw and smoothed with a wood rasp. The mortises should then be laid out according to the sketch and cut, by first boring 3/4-in. holes and finishing with a chisel, being careful to keep all edges clean and free from slivers.

The shelf can now be made by cutting a double-key tenon at each end to fit the end pieces. The space between the two tenons at each end can be cut out with a bracket saw and finished with a rasp. The key holes should be mortised as shown in the sketch. The trough pieces are made in a similar manner, care being taken to have all tenons and mortises perfectly square and a good fit, so the trough when assembled will have a neat and workmanlike appearance. The trough can be finished in any one of the many mission finishes which are supplied by the trade for this purpose.

AN OAK SERVING TABLE

The serving table is another useful piece of furniture that can be made in mission style. This table should be made in quarter-sawed oak and stained very light. The stock order is as follows:

2 posts, 2 by 2 by 37 in., S-4-S.
2 posts, 2 by 2 by 31 in., S-4-S.
1 top, 1 by 21 by 40 in., S-2-S.
2 side rails, 3/4 by 3 by 34-1/2 in., S-2-S.
4 end rails, 3/4 by 3 by 15-1/2 in., S-2-S.
1 back panel, 3/4 by 4 by 34-1/2 in., S-2-S.
1 stretcher, 1 by 5 by 36-1/2 in., S-4-S.
1 slat, 1/2 by 1-1/2 by 36 in., S-4-S.

The four posts are ordered 1 in. longer than necessary for squaring to length and the two back posts should be chamfered 1/4 in. on top, as they are the longest and project above the back panel. All of the posts are cut tapering for a space of 4 in. from the bottom ends. Mortises in the posts and tenons on the rails are laid out and cut as shown by the dimensions in the drawing. These parts are then well glued and put together. The top, which should be of well seasoned wood, is cut to fit around the back posts so the back edge and the back side of the posts are flush. The back panel is placed in mortises cut in the corners of the back posts. This is done so the back surface of the panel will be flush the same as the edge of the top. The slat is fastened with round-headed brass screws on the front of the two back posts about half way between the top and the ends of the posts.

The top may be fastened to the rails by one of two methods. One way is to use a small button made of wood and so mortised as to set in the rails and then fastened to the top with screws. About six of these buttons will be sufficient to hold the top in place. The other method is to bore a hole slanting on the inside of the rails, directing the bit toward the top, which will make a seat—if not cut too deep—for a screw that can be turned direct into the top.

The glue must be removed from about the joints and the surfaces smoothed over with fine sandpaper before applying the stain. The directions for staining will be found on the can in which it is sold. The grain of the wood will show up well if the surface is given a dull waxed finish after staining.

AN UMBRELLA STAND

The umbrella stand shown in the accompanying illustration will be found quite appropriate for the hall or reception room that is furnished in mission style. It can be made of any of the furniture woods, but quarter-sawed oak gives the best results. The stock necessary to make this stand can be secured from the mill ready cut to length, squared and sanded, and is given in the following list:

4 posts, 1-1/2 by 1-1/2 by 28 in., S-4-S.
4 top rails, 7/8 by 2 by 10 in., S-2-S.
4 lower rails, 7/8 by 3 by 10 in., S-2-S.
4 slats, 3/8 by 3 by 20 in., S-2-S.
1 bottom, 7/8 by 10 by 10 in.

First square up the posts and bevel the tops as shown in the detail sketch. Place them side by side, on a flat surface with the ends square and lay out the mortises with a try-square on all four pieces at the same time. This will insure your getting them all straight and of the same height. Now lay out the tenons on the rails in the same manner and cut them to fit the mortises in the posts. Mortises should also be cut in the rails for the ends of the side slats as shown. Try all the joints and see that they fit tight and square. Glue two sides of the stand together and let them dry for at least 24 hours, then glue the remaining parts, being careful to get everything together perfectly square.

The bottom board can now be fitted in place. It should have a hole cut in it for the drip pan. The pan should be about 6 or 7 in. in diameter. One suitable for the purpose can be purchased in any hardware store. The bottom board can be fastened to the rails with nails driven from the under side, or cleats can be nailed to the rails for it to rest upon.

When the stand is complete, scrape all glue from about the joints and go over the whole with fine sandpaper, removing all rough spots. Apply the finish you like best, or the one that will match your other furniture.

Should the builder want an entire hand-made stand, the drip pan may be beaten into shape from sheet brass or copper. This kind of work is known as repoussé. After beating the pan into shape, it can be finished in antique, old copper or given a polished surface, as desired.

A CHAFING DISH BUFFET

The chafing-dish buffet is something very convenient and attractive for the dining room. For the best effect it should be made of quartered oak, stained brown or weathered and trimmed with brass hardware.

To save a great deal of uninteresting labor, secure the following pieces of stock, surfaced on four sides and cut to length:

4 legs, 1-1/2 by 1-1/2 by 36 in., S-4-S.
4 rails, 7/8 by 4 by 10 in., S-4-S.
2 rails, 7/8 by 3 by 10 in., S-4-S.
2 panels, 3/8 by 9-3/8 by 9-1/2 in., S-4-S.
1 panel, 3/8 by 6-1/2 by 9-1/2 in., S-4-S.
2 shelves, 7/8 by 12 by 19 in., S-4-S.
1 top, 7/8 by 16 by 20 in., S-4-S.
2 stiles for door, 7/8 by 2 by 12 in., S-4-S.
2 rails for door, 7/8 by 3 by 10 in., S-4-S.
1 back, 7/8 by 12 by 13 in., S-4-S.
8 slats, 3/8 by 1 by 8 in., S-4-S.

Begin the work on the rails for the sides of the stand. Have them all squared up to exactly the same length and to the correct width and thickness. Mark the tenons on the ends of each and cut them with a saw and chisel.

When this is finished, try the legs to see that they are all the same length and that their surfaces are square with each other. Next mark the mortises in the legs for the tenons of the rails. To make the mortises, first bore to depth with a bit 1/8 in, smaller than the width of the mortise and cut to the line with a chisel.

Before gluing up the sides, cut the mortises in two lower rails for the tenons on the ends of the shelves. These tenons, with the smaller mortises in them for the keys, should be cut first. Square up the two side panels and cut grooves 3/8 in. wide and 1/4 in. deep for them in the rails and part of the legs.

Make the eight slats 8 in. long, 1 in. wide and 3/8 in. thick, and cut mortises for them in the two upper rails.

The two sides of the buffet are now ready to be glued up and clamped. While the glue on these is setting, make the door. The rails are mortised into the stiles 1/2 in. and both are grooved to receive the panel. It is best to get the stock a little full for the door so that it may be made up a little larger than necessary and planed down to fit.

There only remains to fit in the shelves and fasten the top and back. The top and back are held with screws as shown in sketch.

Taper the keys only slightly, otherwise they will keep working loose.

Stain with two coats of weathered oak, give one coat of thin shellac to fix the stain and two coats of wax for a soft-gloss finish.

PART III. A WRITING DESK

A WRITING DESK

The desk shown in the illustration was made of plain-sawed white oak. The copper lighting fixtures were made by the amateur as were the hinges and the drawer pulls. The doors are fitted with art-glass panels. The following stock list is needed:

1 top, 3/4 by 22-1/2 by 41 in., S-2-S.
4 posts, 2 by 2 by 31 in., S-4-S.
2 rails, 3/4 by 6-1/4 by 19 in., S-2-S.
2 rails, 3/4 by 6-1/4 by 35 in., S-2-S.
2 rails, 3/4 by 3-1/4 by 19 in., S-2-S.
1 stretcher, 3/4 by 3-1/4 by 35 in., S-2-S.
2 drawer fronts, 3/4 by 4-1/4 by 14 in., S-2-S.
4 drawer sides, 1/2 by 4-1/4 by 19 in., S-2-S.
2 drawer backs, 3/8 by 4 by 14 in., S-2-S.
2 drawer bottoms, 3/8 by 19 by 14 in., S-2-S.
4 slides, 3/4 by 2-1/2 by 19 in., S-2-S.
8 guides, 3/4 by 2 by 10 in., S-2-S.
2 cabinet posts, 1 by 1 by 16 in., S-4-S.
4 cabinet posts, 1 by 1 by 11 in., S-4-S.
1 back, 3/4 by 16 by 35 in., S-2-S.
1 shelf, 3/4 by 8 by 35 in., S-2-S.
2 shelves, 3/4 by 8 by 15 in., S-2-S.
4 door pieces, 5/8 by 1 by 15 in., S-2-S.
8 door pieces, 5/8 by 1 by 4 in., S-2-S.

Square the legs to length and lay out and cut the mortises thereon. Lay off the tenons on the rails, after having squared the rails to length and width, and cut them.

Work up the top of the table and then the drawer stock and cabinet. Assemble the ends of the frame first, using good hot glue and enough clamps to hold the parts together properly. After the glue has hardened on these, the clamps may be removed and the front, back rails and the stretcher assembled.

While the glue is hardening on the main frame the top cabinet may be built and assembled. This cabinet is detachable from the table proper and is to be held in place by means of cleats upon the back. These cleats are not specified in the bill; they may be obtained from scrap stock.

For a piece of woodwork of this style some of the softer browns of the mission stains will be most appropriate. After all parts have been thoroughly cleaned by scraping and sandpapering, a stain may be applied. Allow this to dry, then sand it lightly and apply a thin coat of shellac. Sand the shellac lightly and apply a filler of a color to match the stain, but darker in tone, of course. Clean off the surplus in the usual manner and then apply a coat of shellac. Sand this lightly and apply several coats of some good polishing wax.

MUSIC RACK AND BOOKSTAND

The illustration shows a very handy music and bookstand, which also can be used at the bedside as a reading stand. The following list of material will be required for construction:

1 standard, 1-1/8 by 1-1/8 by 37 in., S-4-S.
1 horizontal, 1-1/8 by 1-1/8 by 15 in., S-4-S.
1 crosspiece, 1-1/8 by 1-1/8 by 14 in., S-4-S.
1 crosspiece, 1-1/8 by 1-1/8 by 12 in., S-4-S.
2 braces, 1-1/8 by 1-1/8 by 9 in., S-4-S.
1 board, 1/2 by 8 by 13 in., S-2-S.
4 blocks, 1-1/8 in. square.
2 gauge clamps.
1 strip, 1/2 by 1 by 13 in., S-2-S.
8 round-head brass screws.
1 brass rod, 1/4 in. in diameter and 12 in, long.
1 brass piece, 1/4 by 3/4 by 10 in.

Cut a tenon on the lower end of the upright and make a mortise in the center of the long crosspiece to receive the tenon. The horizontal has tenons cut on both ends which fit into mortises cut in the sides of both crosspieces. The upper corners on the ends of both crosspieces are cut sloping on a 45-deg. angle. The blocks for the feet are attached to the under side and at the end on each crosspiece with screws and hot glue, the screw heads being sunk so that they will not catch on carpets or mar the floor. The braces are attached with round-head screws after they are cut on each end to fit the standard and crosspiece.

The book rest is cut from the board. The openings are made by sawing the pieces out with a coping saw, and the edges are dressed up with a sharp chisel. The lip strip is then glued to the lower edge of the board.

One end of the board is now fitted into a slot cut in one of the gauge clamps. The slot must be cut at the right angle to give the desired slope to the book rest. The gauge clamps are joined with two small square strips of oak as shown. The small rod brace is flattened at both ends and a hole drilled in each to fasten it with screws as shown. The brass strip is bent in the middle at right angles and drilled to receive screws for fastening it in the corner of the upright and horizontal pieces.

A DICTIONARY AND MAGAZINE STAND

The accompanying picture shows a stand that is intended primarily for holding a large-size dictionary. The shelves may be utilized for holding books, magazines or sheet music. It will stand wear best if made of some hard wood, such as oak. Of the soft woods chestnut has the best grain for finishing, being hardly distinguishable from red oak.

The following pieces will be necessary:

2 sides, 3/4 by 16 by 38-1/2 in., S-4-S.
1 shelf, 3/4 by 15-1/2 by 21 in., S-2-S.
1 shelf, 3/4 by 14 by 17 in., S-2-S.
1 shelf, 3/4 by 13-1/2 by 21 in., S-2-S.
1 top, 3/4 by 13 by 17 in., S-2-S.
1 lip, 3/8 by 3/4 by 17 in., S-4-S.
8 keys, 3/4 by 1 by 3-1/2 in., S-2-S.

Begin work on the sides by preparing a joint edge on each piece and from this square up the lower ends and square lines across the inner surfaces to indicate the positions of the lower edges of the shelves.

Next, smooth off the mill marks from the broad surfaces of the shelves and square them to size on one edge and the two ends.

Return to the side pieces and lay out the outline, but do not cut to these lines until the gains and mortises which are to receive the ends of the shelves and their tenons have been laid out and cut. Laying out these outlines at this time is done so as to give the exact width the shelves are to have. These dimensions can be determined by measuring across the sides between the outlines at the points where the shelves are to be placed.

The shelves which have no tenons are to be let into the sides 1/4 in. They should be shouldered 1/2 in. back from the edge so that the groove will not show on the face.

The lip on the front of the top shelf may be fastened by means of very small brads, the heads of which should be covered with putty, colored to match the finish.

A suitable finish may be obtained as follows:

First see that all the mill marks are removed, using a smooth plane and steel scraper and sandpaper, then apply a coat of cathedral-oak water stain. When dry, sandpaper lightly, using No. 00 paper. Apply a second coat of stain, diluting it by the addition of an equal volume of water. This is to produce a stronger contrast. Sand this lightly and put on a very thin coat of shellac to bind the filler and to prevent the stain in the filler which follows from discoloring the high lights. Sand this lightly and put on a coat of paste filler according to the directions that will be found on the can. This filler should be colored in the following proportions: Light paste filler, 20 lb.; Van Dyke brown, 1 lb. After the filler has hardened, sand it lightly and put on a coat of orange shellac. Follow this with several coats of some good rubbing varnish. The first coats should be rubbed with haircloth or curled hair, and the last with powdered pumice stone and raw linseed or crude oil.

A LEATHER BACK ARM CHAIR

A mission arm chair of simple design and construction is shown in the accompanying illustration. This chair is suitable for any room of the house and can be made of wood to match other furniture. Quarter-sawed oak is the wood most generally used, and it is also very easy to obtain. The stock can be ordered from the mill, cut to length, squared and sanded. Following is a list of the material that will be needed:

2 front legs, 2 by 2 by 26-3/4 in.
2 back legs, 2 by 4 by 43 in.
2 arm rests, 1 by 4 by 26 in.
5 rails, 3/4 by 4 by 21-1/2 in.
5 rails, 3/4 by 2 by 2-1/2 in. .
2 back pieces, 3/4 by 2 by 16-1/2 in.
1 piece leather, 31 in, square.
1 piece burlap, 28 in, square.
2 pieces leather, 13 by 18 in.
2 pieces burlap, 13 by 18 in.
1 box 8 oz. tacks.
5-1/2 doz. ornamental nails.

Start with the front legs. Cut a tenon 1-1/4 in. square and 3/4 in, long on one end to fit the arm rests. The mortises for the side rails are cut 1/2 in. wide and 7/8 in, deep. The tenons on the rails are cut to fit these mortises, care being taken to get them all the same length between shoulders. The back legs are cut with an offset of 2 in. as shown in the detail drawing and also have mortises cut in them for the back crosspieces. The upright pieces in the back are fastened into the crosspieces by means of tenons and mortises, and should be in place when the crosspieces are fastened to the legs.

The arms are cut from the 1 by 4 by 26-in. pieces. Be careful to get them so they will pair. The outside edge can be either curved or straight as desired. The front ends of the arms are held in place by mortises which fit over the tenons on the ends of the front legs, while the back ends are held in place by round-headed screws as shown.

The chair is now ready to be glued. Be sure to get the parts together perfectly square, and when dry scrape off all surplus glue around the joints, for stain will not adhere to glue and a white spot will be the result of failing to remove it. Go over the parts carefully with fine sandpaper and remove all rough marks. Then apply the stain you wish to use. To make the seat, first fit boards in the bottom and nail them to the side rails as shown. Fill the space with hair or elastic cotton felt to about 3 in. above the edge of the rails. Bind this down tightly with a piece of burlap and tack the edges to the rails. Cut out the corners of the burlap so that it will fit about the posts. Put the leather on over this and tack the edges to the bottoms of the rails. Then finish with the ornamental nails as shown.

To finish the back, first tack a piece of burlap over the opening, then place a layer of hair or cotton felt on this about 1 in. thick. Stretch the leather over this and fasten with ornamental nails. The back side is finished in the same manner, except that the hair is omitted.

A WALL SHELF

Coarse-grained woods make up into furniture and take a more satisfactory finish than close-grained woods. For this reason chestnut or oak is suggested for this shelf. Chestnut has a beautiful grain and is soft and easily worked.

There will be needed the following pieces:
Sides, 2 pieces, 3/4 by 7-1/4 by 16-1/2 in., S-2-S.
Lower shelf, 1 piece, 3/4 by 6-1/4 by 30-1/2 in., S-2-S.
Upper shelf, 1 piece, 3/4 by 4-3/4 by 30-1/2 in., S 2 S.
Lower back, 1 piece, 3/8 by 3-1/2 by 30-1/2 in., S-2-S.
Upper back, 1 piece, 3/8 by 3 by 30-1/2 in., S-2-S.

In making out this stock bill the pieces have been specified 1/4 in. wider and 1/2 in. longer than the finished piece is to be to allow for squaring up. The thicknesses are specified mill-planed exact so that all that is necessary is to merely plane off the mill-marks from the two broad surfaces.

It is quite possible that one may have a particular space or a particular set of books to place in the shelf. In such a case the length of the horizontals should be lengthened or shortened to meet the particular demands when ordering the lumber.

Begin work by squaring the horizontals to size. They are to be all of the same length. Next shape up the end pieces. The amount of slope for the front edges is indicated on the drawing. After all these pieces have been squared up and the mill-marks removed, the dadoes or grooves and gains may be laid out and cut.

Beginners are prone to underestimate the importance of getting all the mill-marks off before putting on any finish. When boards are planed at the mill the planing is done by means of two or four knives revolving above or below the board—sometimes both above and below at the same time. These knives leave the surfaces filled with little ridges and hollows across the grain. These hollows, though they are hardly visible to the eye on the unfinished surface, show up as ugly streaks upon the surface after it has had a finish of stain and filler applied.

The joints here used are typical and the beginner can readily find how they are to be made from any good book on wood-working.

There are several ways of fastening the parts. They may be fastened by means of round-head blued screws. They may be fastened with carriage screws. The one in the illustration was put together with ordinary wire nails and the heads of these covered with ornamental heads to represent old-fashioned hand-wrought nails.

It will be found easier to apply the finish of stain and filler before the parts are assembled. A suitable finish is obtained as follows: After the parts are thoroughly sanded, put on a coat of Filipino water stain, wiping it off with an old cloth before it has had time to soak into the wood very much. Allow this to dry. Then sand lightly, using No. 00 paper, after which fill the pores of the wood with a black paste filler—directions will be found on the can. Follow this, when hardened, with several coats of floor wax.

A PEDESTAL

The pedestal shown in the accompanying illustration is another piece of furniture that can be made in the mission style. It is very simple in design and construction, and can be made by anyone who has a few simple tools and a slight knowledge of their use. It is best to make it of quarter-sawed oak as this is the most easily procured wood and also looks the best when finished. If you order the material from the mill ready cut to length, squared and sanded, much hard labor will be saved. Following is a list of the material needed:

1 top, 3/4 by 12 by 12 in., S-1-S.
1 bottom, 3/4 by 12 by 12 in., S-1-S
8 pieces, 3/4 by 2 by 11 in.
2 sides, 3/4 by 5 by 26 in., S-1-S.
2 sides, 3/4 by 3-1/2 by 26 in.

1 piece, 3/4 by 6 by 6 in.

4 blocks, 1 in. square.

Having the boards for the post cut to the proper length and square, nail them together as shown in the detail drawing. Use finishing nails, then set the heads and fill the holes with putty. Next, nail the 3/4 by 6-in. piece on one end of the post leaving the edges projecting even on all sides. Pick out the best board for the top. On the under side and 1/2. in. in from the edges, nail four of the 3/4 by 2 by 11-in. pieces which have been previously mitered as shown in the plan view. Now fasten this top to the post by nailing through the projecting edge of the top piece into the top board. Be careful to get this top on square with the post and exactly in center.

The bottom board is made in the same manner as the top board and is nailed to the lower end of the post as shown. Four 1-in. square blocks should be fastened to the bottom for the pedestal to rest on.

When complete, sandpaper smooth and apply any one of the many mission stains that are supplied by the trade for this purpose.

After staining the wood, the surface can be given a polished or dull finish, as desired. Mission furniture requires a dull finish, and this may be obtained by applying a coat of wax, well rubbed on the wood.

PART IV. MAGAZINE RACK

MAGAZINE RACK

The accompanying cut shows a magazine rack that will find favor with many amateur wood-workers on account of its simplicity in design and its rich, massive appearance when properly finished. It is so constructed that each piece may be polished, stained and finished before it is finally put together. Quarter-sawed oak is the best wood to use. Plain-sawed oak looks well, but it is more liable to warp than quarter-sawed and this is quite an element in pieces as wide as the ones here used. Following is a list of the material needed:

4 posts, 2 by 2 by 40 in., S-4-S.

5 shelves, 1 by 14 by 24 in., S-2-S.

20 F.H. screws, 2 in. long.

Considerable labor can be saved if the material be ordered from the mill ready cut to length, squared and sanded. The corner posts should be made first. The most convenient and accurate method of laying out the mortises is to square one end of each post and lay them on the bench flat, with the squared ends even with each other; then clamp them securely and lay out the mortises on one side across all four pieces at once; then loosen the clamp and project the marks to the other side with a try-square. Now saw along these marks, making each cut just deep enough to bring the mortises diagonally across the piece from one corner to the opposite corner as shown in the detail sketch. Be careful not to get the mortises wider than the shelves are thick. Bevel the tops of the posts as shown.

See that the ends of the shelves are square and smooth, then set a scratch gauge so that the scriber is just 2 in. from the face of the block and mark this distance off each way from the corner of the shelves. Saw these corners diagonally across as shown, being careful not to saw off too much.

The parts can now be assembled. Place all the parts in position, then pass a rope around each end and twist it up tightly with a small stick. If this is properly done, you can now pick up the rack and handle it in any way you wish. The screws can now be put in the corners. You can use flat-head screws and plug the holes, or you can use round-head blue screws and let the heads project. After the screws are all in, dress off all unevenness where the shelves are mortised into the posts, then mark each shelf and post so that you can put it together again after the parts are finished. Take the rack apart and transfer the marks to some part of the mortises and shelves that will not be covered with the finish you intend to put on. Apply the finish you wish to use and when the parts are thoroughly dry they can be reassembled and your rack will be complete.

A HALL TREE

When making the hall tree as shown in the accompanying illustration use quarter-sawed oak if possible, as this wood is the most suitable for finishing in the different mission stains. This is a very useful and attractive piece of mission furniture and is also very easy to construct. The stock can be purchased ready cut to length, mill-planed and sandpapered on four sides as given in the following list:
1 post, 2 by 2 by 59 in.
4 posts, 2 by 2 by 10 in.
8 braces, 7/8 by 2 by 7-1/2 in.
4 arms, 7/8 by 2 by 5-3/4 in.

First square up all the posts and bevel them at the tops as shown. Then cut the mortises making them 1/2 in. wide and 7/8 in. deep. Cut the tenons on the braces to fit these mortises. Be careful to get the distance between the shoulders of the braces all of the same length. A good way to do this is to place them all side by side on a flat surface with the ends square and lay them all out at once. The top arms can be made in the same manner. The tenons should fit good and tight in all the posts.

The parts can now be glued and clamped together. When they are dry, scrape all the surplus glue from about the joints and go over the whole with fine sandpaper, removing all rough spots. Apply the finish you like best or the one that will match your other furniture. Purchase a few hooks at a hardware store and fasten in the upper arms as shown, and the hall tree is complete.

A TABLE FOR THE DEN

The table shown in the accompanying sketch is especially appropriate for the den; it might be used in any other part of the house as well. It may be built of plain-sawed red oak, or of quarter-sawed white oak. The wood should be thoroughly seasoned and devoid of imperfections.

Order the material as follows:

1 top piece, 3/4 in. thick by 36 in. square, S-2-S.

4 legs, 2-1/2 in. square by 30 in. long, S-4-S.

2 upper horizontals, 1-1/8 by 2 by 36 in., S-4-S.

2 lower horizontals, 3/4 by 2-1/2 by 35 in., S-4-S.

4 keys, 1/2 by 1 by 5 in., S-2-S.

Lay out and cut the circular top first. Next cut the four legs to length. To get the slopes for the ends of the legs and the shoulders of the tenons, lay out a full-sized drawing in pencil and lay the bevel along these lines, adjusting the parts to the lines.

The top horizontals have grooves cut on either side to allow the posts to "set in." This is to give the frame more rigidity. The lower horizontals or stretchers are to be tenoned through the posts and keyed. That the keys may be alike in size, a good plan is to make them first, then make the mortises in the stretchers to correspond. Work the keys to the proper thickness, unless they were ordered so, then to length and joint one edge straight and square. Next lay off across the key the lines A and B of the drawing so that A shall measure 1/2 in. and B 3/8 in. Draw a sloping line through these points and work this edge of the key to size and shape. Round the top of the key as shown. Then mortise, in the tenon, for the key can then be laid out to 1/2 in. for the top opening and 3/8 in. for the bottom.

The most satisfactory finish for mission designs, and the easiest to apply, is wax. It is an old finish that was superseded by varnish. Our ancestors used to make wax polish by "cutting" beeswax with turpentine. Cut up the beeswax and add to it about one-third its volume of turpentine. Heat to the boiling point in a double boiler. Or, melt a quantity of beeswax and to this add an equal volume of turpentine. Care must be taken that the turpentine shall not catch fire.

Rapid drying and hardening waxes can be purchased now-a-days. They require a smooth surface and a thin application for a successful result. Too much wax upon a rough surface will produce very ugly, white, chalk-like spottings as the wax dries. These are especially noticeable upon dark finishes. Waxes colored black overcome this, but are not necessary if the ordinary wax is properly applied. 1—Stain the wood, if a very dark finish is desired. 2—If the wood is coarse grained, put on one or two coats of paste filler and rub it off carefully, that a smooth surface may be prepared. Allow the stain 12 hours in which to dry, also each coat of filler. 3—With a soft cloth apply as thin a coating of wax as can be and still cover the wood. Wax is in paste form. 4—Allow this to stand five or ten minutes, then rub briskly with a soft dry cloth to polish. 5—Let stand 24 hours, then apply another coat.

A BURLAP COVERED WINDOW SEAT

A portable window seat of neat appearance, which is designed to take the place of a cedar chest, is shown in the accompanying sketch. If care is taken to make the joints fit well, the box will be practically airtight and mothproof, providing a place in which to store extra bedding or furs. The following list of materials will be needed:

36 ft. 1-in. thick cedar boards for the box.

1 piece pine, 2 by 2 in. by 12 ft. long.

32 ft. of 1/4 by 2-in. oak strips.

54 ft. of 1/4 by 1-in. oak strips.

16 doz. R.H. 3/4-in, long brass screws.

1 piece green burlap, 24 by 48 in.

2 pieces green burlap, 20 by 44 in.

2 pieces green burlap, 20 by 20 in.

20 pieces red burlap, 3-1/4 in. square.

The box as shown in Fig. 1 is made first. Nail the sides and the bottom to the ends, being careful to get the box perfectly square. The corners can be dovetailed together if desired. The extra time it takes in making the dovetailed joints will greatly add to the durability of the box. The box can be made much stronger by nailing the sides and ends to posts 2 in. square placed on the inside. Cleats should also be placed on the inside, at the bottom, as shown. Fasten four blocks, 2 in. square, to the bottom for the box to rest upon. These can be attached with long screws run through from the bottom of the box.

The green burlap is glued to the outside of the box. Be careful not to apply too much glue on the burlap, or it will soak through. This should be tried out on a scrap piece, and when the proper application of glue is ascertained, applied to one side of the burlap and stuck on the box. Place the cloth on so . the weave will run in the same direction on all sides. The oak slats are cut and fit over the burlap as shown in Fig. 2. Care should be taken to make the mitered joints a tight fit. After the miters are all cut and the location of the squares, found, they are marked so that pieces of red burlap may be placed over the green before the slats are fastened permanently. The slats are put in place over the burlap and fastened with small brass screws.

Cover the top or lid with green burlap, allowing the edges to lap over the ends and sides and fasten under the side strips. This top can be stuffed with excelsior, if desired, and tacks with large heads driven in to hold it in place. The slats can be stained any color to suit the maker. They should be removed from the box when being stained so as not to spot or stain the burlap.

QUARTER SAWED OAK SETTEE

The mission settee shown in the accompanying picture should be made of quarter-sawed white oak. The material needed will be as follows:

4 posts, 3-1/4 by 3-1/4 by 36-1/2 in., S-4-S.
4 end rails, 1-1/2 by 5 by 32 in., S-4-S.
12 end slats, 5/8 by 3-1/2 by 24 in., S-4-S.
1 front rail, 1-1/2 by 7 by 87 in., S-4-S.
1 lower back rail, 1-1/2 by 9 by 87 in., S-4-S.
1 upper back rail, 1-1/2 by 12 by 87 in., S-4-S.
2 cleats for seat frame, 1-1/2 by 2 by 82 in., S-4-S.
2 cleats for seat frame, 1-1/2 by 2 by 32 in., S-4-S.

On account of the unusual width of the pieces that go into the makeup of this settee, it will be necessary to have the wood thoroughly seasoned before putting them together, otherwise shrinkage will cause them to crack open.

Begin work by making the ends of the settee first. Cut the posts to length, chamfering both top and bottoms somewhat so that they shall not splinter or cause injury to the hands. Next lay out and cut the mortises as shown on the drawing. With the posts finished, lay out the end rails, cutting the tenons and the mortises into which the ends of the slats are to be fitted.

It should be noted that the drawing calls for the "setting in" of the whole of the ends of the slats, there being no shoulders. This is much easier and gives just as satisfactory a result, provided the sides of the mortises are carefully cut.

Thoroughly scrape and sandpaper all these parts and then put the ends together. In addition to the glue it will be well to through pin each of the tenons and mortises. These pins may be put in flush and permanent on the ends of the settee. On the side rails, however, the pins are to be allowed to project so that they can be removed, and no glue is used in the joint.

While the glue of the ends is hardening, prepare the rails of front and back. Scrape and sandpaper these and when the clamps can be removed from the ends put the whole frame together. The ends of all projecting tenons are chamfered.

The illustration shows a loose leather cushion. There is quite a variety of materials out of which such a cushion can be made. The best, of course, is leather. In the highest class of furniture where loose cushions are used, the seat base is formed by solidly mortising a frame together on which is woven a heavy cane seating. This in turn is fastened to the inside of the piece of furniture, and the cushions when placed upon it make a very comfortable seat. The stock bill for this settee calls for such a frame. Wood slats may be substituted if desired.

This piece of furniture will look well if finished in weathered oak. See that all glue is removed from the surface, and that the wood is clean and smooth, and apply a coat of weathered oak oil stain. Sandpaper this lightly with No. 00 paper when the stain has thoroughly dried, and put on a coat of lackluster or an equivalent.

A SCREEN

In selecting or making up mission furniture for the home, a screen is necessary sometimes to add to the appearance of a room. The screen shown in the accompanying illustration consists of a few parts which are easily put together. The stock can be bought of any planing mill planed, sanded and cut to the proper lengths. The cloth, which should be of dark color, can be purchased at a dry goods store. The following list of material will be needed.

6 posts, 1 in. square by 65 in.
6 rails, 3/4 in. square by 18 in.
6 rails, 1/2 in. square by 18 in.
3 panels, 1/4 by 3 by 18 in.
6 yd. of cloth.
4 double-acting hinges.
2 doz. 2-1/2-in. slender screws.

Cut or plow a groove 1/4 in. wide and 1/4 in. deep in the center of one surface on each of the 3/4-in. rails. Cut out the ends with a compass saw. The five holes are bored with a 1-in. bit. The edges of these panels are inserted in the grooves of the 3/4-in. rails, using plenty of good glue.

When the glue has dried for at least 24 hours the screen frame can be put together. Holes for the screws should be bored through the posts where the 3/4-in. rails are joined and a screw turned into the end grain of each rail.

Scrape off all the surplus glue and sandpaper all the parts well. When this is done the finish can be applied. Any one of the mission stains can be used and finished with wax and polished.

The cloth is cut to length, a hem sewed on each end and one 1/2-in. rail put through each hem. Place the top rail in position and screw it fast. Stretch the cloth tight and fasten the lower 1/2-in. rail with screws at the bottom. Each section of the screen is finished in the same way.

The hinges are attached about 4 in. from each end of the posts in the same manner as hanging a door.

The sections can be made up in various ways to suit the builder. Instead of using cloth, heavy paste-board, or board made up to take the place of plaster on walls of dwellings, may be substituted, thus forming a ground that will take paint and bronze decorations. A piece of this material can be easily cut to fit the opening in each section.

PART V. A MISSION BOOKRACK

A MISSION BOOKRACK

The accompanying sketch shows a bookrack designed strictly along mission lines. Enough stock may be found among the scrap, as no piece is over 1 in, in width or thickness. If stock is not on hand, secure the following, cut to exact lengths:

2 stretchers, 1 by 1 by 20 in., S-4-S.

4 posts, 1 by 1 by 7-1/2 in., S-4-S.

4 rails, 1 by 1 by 7 in., S-4-S.

8 slats, 1/2 by 1/2 by 3-1/2 in., S-4-S.

Arrange the pieces as they are to be in the finished rack and number both parts of each joint. There will be twelve lap joints, and great care must be taken to mark them accurately and to cut to exactly half the depth of each piece.

First fit the posts and rails of the ends. To mark the width of each notch, lay the piece which is to fit into the notch upon it and thus get the exact size. Knife lines must be used for the width and light gauge lines for the depth of each notch.

Next lay out and cut joints between the stretchers and ends.

In each end there are four slats which should be mortised into the rails 1/4 in. Glue the pieces in place and clamp them with handscrews.

A rubber-headed tack in the bottom of each post will prevent the marring of the surface upon which the rack is to rest.

Mission, weathered or fumed-oak stain will look well. A waxed finish should be used. Before applying the wax, it is well to use a very thin coat of shellac as a foundation. Let this coat stand for a few hours and allow an interval of at least an hour between applying the coats of wax.

Should the rack wind a little, it may be remedied by cutting off part of two diagonally opposite racks.

A ROUND EXTENSION DINING TABLE

This extension table should be made of some hard wood, preferably white oak. It will be a difficult matter to secure legs of the sizes indicated in solid pieces of clear stock. It will be possible, however, to secure them veneered upon white-pine cores. If the veneering is properly done these will serve the purpose very well, the lighter weight, due to the white-pine core, being an advantage. The circular facing is best made by first sawing a segment of the circle of the size wanted and then veneering the outer surface of this. Order the following stock:

4 legs, 3 by 3 by 30-1/2 in., S-4-S.

1 leg, 5 by 5 by 30-1/2 in., S-4-S.

4 rails, 1-1/8 by 5 by 23 in., S-2-S.

4 facing segments, 1-1/8 by 3-1/4 in. on a 24-in. radius.

1 top, 1-1/8 in. thick on a 27-in. radius, S-2-S;

3 extra boards, 1-1/8 by 12 by 55 in., S-2-S.

4 slides, 1-1/8 by 2-3/4 by 36-1/2 in., S-4-S, maple.

2 slides, 1-1/4 by 2-3/4 by 36-1/2 in., S-4-S, maple.

4 frame pieces, 7/8 by 3 by 9 in., S-4-S, maple.

2 frame pieces, 7/8 by 6 by 28 in., S-4-S, maple.

2 frame pieces, 7/8 by 4 by 23-1/2 in., S-4-S, maple.

There are various ways of arranging the slides to work one with the other. Several patented devices are on the market that permit a ready adjustment with but little effort and are used extensively by commercial manufacturers. The amateur will do well to secure a set before he undertakes to work these slides to shape.

Prepare the legs by cutting them to length. Lay out and work the mortises. The ends of the facings are to be tenoned and housed into the posts. Prepare the rails by cutting the tenons and shaping the lower edges as shown in the drawing. Prepare the top. After this, assemble this much of the frame, using plenty of clamps and good hot glue.

Next get the under frame and the slides ready and attach them as shown. There will be needed plenty of glue blocks for reinforcing the facing where it is fastened to the top, etc.

For a finish, apply a filler colored, as desired. Upon this, after it has hardened and been sanded with No. 00 paper, apply a coat of shellac. Upon the shellac apply successively several coats of some good rubbing varnish. Rub the first coats with haircloth and the final coat with pulverized pumice and crude or linseed oil.

If an effect is wanted that will contrast, stain the wood first with a water stain. Sand this lightly when dry, then apply a second coat of stain diluted one-half with water. Again sand and then apply a thin coat of shellac. Sand this lightly, and apply the filler and the varnish as described above.

AN ARM DINING CHAIR

This armchair will look well if made of plain-sawed oak. Quarter-sawed oak might be used, or black walnut if desired. The stock bill specifies the various parts mill-planed to size as far as possible. If some amateur craftsman should prefer to do his own surfacing, thereby saving somewhat on the expense, he should add 1/4 in. to the width of each piece, providing the stock is mill-planed to thickness. It is hardly profitable to get stock entirely in the rough if the work is to be done by hand. The following is the stock bill:

2 front posts, 1-3/4 by 1-3/4 by 25 in., S-4-S.
1 piece for back posts, 1-3/4 by 6 by 43 in., S-2-S.
2 arm pieces, 7/8 by 4 by 24-1/2 in., S-4-S.
2 seat rails, 1 by 2-1/2 by 22 in., S-4-S.
2 seat rails, 1 by 2-1/2 by 24 in., S-4-S.
4 lower side rails, 5/8 by 1-1/2 by 22 in., S-4-S.
2 front and back lower rails, 5/8 by 2-3/4 by 24 in., S-4-S.
1 back rail, 3/4 by 2-1/4 by 24 in., S-4-S.
1 back rail, 3/4 by 2-1/2 by 24 in., S-4-S.
2 slats, 3/8 by 2 by 16-1/2 in., S-4-S.
1 slat, 3/8 by 4-1/2 by 16-1/2 in., S-4-S.
2 braces, 7/8 by 2-1/2 by 5-1/2 in., S-2-S.

The design shown is for a chair in which the width of front and back is the same. Also the back leg parallels the front below the seat. In commercial practice the backs are usually made somewhat narrower than the fronts and the back leg is slanted somewhat below the seat as well as above. As this construction necessitates sloping shoulders on all tenons it complicates the problem when the work is not done by machinery. The ambitious amateur may readily get the proportion of slant by measuring common chairs. For mission effects the chair looks well with front and back the same width.

Prepare the front posts first and then the rear. The rear posts are to be cut from the single piece of stock specified. By proper planning both pieces may be gotten out without trouble. Lay off and cut the mortises.

Saw the rails to length and lay out and cut the tenons. The back rails are to have mortises in their edges to receive the ends of the slats. Instead of tenoning these slats make mortises large enough to receive the whole end—in other words, house the ends.

Shape the two arms, then glue up the back and then the front of the chair. After the glue has set sufficiently, assemble the remainder of the parts.

Thoroughly scrape and sandpaper the parts and then apply the finish.

For a seat, either a leather cushion may be placed upon slats or the bottom may be upholstered in the usual manner, using webbing on heavy canvas, and then felt or hair with a top of canvas and leather; the whole being firmly fastened with tacks and the leather with ornamental nails.

A HALL BENCH

All the stock for this bench should be of 7/8-in. oak, excepting the slats, which may be of a cheaper wood. The following list of lumber will be required to build it:

4 slats, 7/8 by 4 by 17 in., cheap wood.
2 cleats, 7/8 by 1 by 26 in., cheap wood.
4 end rails, 7/8 by 2 by 16-1/4 in., oak, S-2-S.
2 ends, 7/8 by 16 by 16-1/4 in., oak, S-2-S.
2 sides, 7/8 by 4 by 25 in., oak, S-2-S.
2 pieces, 7/8 by 5-1/2 by 25 in., oak, S-2-S.

Start the work by first cutting the two pieces of 7/8 by 5-1/2 by 25-in. material diagonally 1 in. from each corner, thus making the legs. The edges are planed square and the ends should be rounded a little so that there will be no splinters projecting. The legs are mortised 1 in. deep for the side rails. The tenon ends are cut on the rails, care being taken to get the right angle and a good fit. These can now be fastened together, using hot glue on the entire surface of the joint.

While these are drying the ends can be made as shown in the plan. The 3 by 4-in. holes are cut at equal distances apart. Be sure that each end is perfectly square, then glue and dowel the 2-in. strips at each end. The ends are then glued and nailed to the sides, using finishing nails, which are set and the holes filled with colored putty.

The cleats are now fastened, extra care being taken when fastening them over the joints where the legs receive the side rails, as this will help to strengthen the joints. The slats rest on these cleats and are placed at equal distances apart.

The bench is now finished, but before applying the stain, see that all parts are free from glue and are well sandpapered.

The leather cushion should be the loose kind and of a shade to harmonize with the finish.

A SEWING TABLE

This convenient and useful table will be much appreciated by any woman. It has two drawers for sewing material, and two drop leaves to spread the work upon.

The following list of material will be needed for its construction. The sizes given are exact, so if the stock cannot be bought at a mill ready planed and squared, a slight allowance must be made for this.

4 posts, 1-1/4 by 1-1/4 by 27 in., S-4-S.

9 rails, 7/8 by 2 by 14-1/2 in., S-2-S.

1 top, 7/8 by 18 by 18 in., S-2-S.

2 leaves, 7/8 by 10 by 18 in., S-2-S.

2 drawer fronts, 3/4 by 5 by 13-1/2 in., S-2-S.

4 drawer sides, 3/8 by 5 by 13 in., S-2-S.

2 drawer backs, 3/8 by 4-1/8 by 13 in., S-2-S.

2 drawer bottoms, 3/8 by 12-3/4 by 13 in., S-2-S.

4 drawer slides, 7/8 by 2 by 13 in., S-2-S.

3 panels, 3/8 by 9-3/8 by 14 in., S-2-S.

2 brackets, 7/8 by 3 by 4 in., S-2-S.

Have the surfaces of the legs exactly square with each other. The ends must be square with all surfaces, but need not be planed smooth as neither will be seen in the finished table.

Arrange the rails in position. The two rails in each side and back are placed with the 2-in. surface out, while the three in the front have the 2-in. surface up for the drawers to slide upon. Mark the tenons, 1 in. by 3/8 in., with a knife and gauge lines on each end of the rails for the sides and back. Mark the tenons, 3/4 in. by 7/8 in., as shown in the sketch, on each end of front rails. Cut all the tenons with a backsaw and smooth them with a chisel.

Carefully mark the mortises in the legs, taking measurements for each mortise from the tenon which is to go into it. Fit together all rails and legs without glue to detect any errors.

See that the panels for sides and back are squared up true and the surfaces smooth. Mark the grooves for the panels in the side and back rails and legs. Cut the grooves with a chisel or plow plane to a depth of 1/4 in.

Glue up the joints and clamp the two table sides first. While the glue is setting, square up and smooth the top and two leaves perfectly.

Now glue up the whole table, having set in the front and back rails and panel. The drawer slides, two on each side, should next be put in. A nail through them and into each leg will hold them, as there is only the weight of the drawers resting on them. Fasten the top with screws through the rails from the under side. The leaves are attached with two 2-in. butt hinges which must be set in flush with the under surface to prevent a crack showing between the table top and leaf when the latter is raised. The small bracket hinged to the panel supports the open leaf.

The drawers are now made. Allow the side to lap over the front 1/2 in. as shown in sketch and fasten it with nails. The bottom should be let into the sides and front 1/4 in., but must not be nailed to them, because this would cause the drawer to stick, when the bottom expands.

Metal rings or wooden knobs will do well for the drawer pulls.

Stain to any desired shade and finish with a wax if a dull gloss is wanted, or with one coat of shellac and two coats of varnish for a highly polished surface.

A SIDE CHAIR

A companion piece to the chair with arms and the sideboard is the side chair illustrated herewith. It should be made of the same kind of wood and finished to correspond with the armchair. Order the following stock list:

2 front posts, 1-1/2 by 1-1/2 by 18-1/2 in., S-4-S.

1 piece for back posts, 1-1/2 by 5-1/2 by 38-1/2 in., S-2-S.

4 seat rails, 1 by 2 by 17 in., S-4-S.

4 lower side rails, 5/8 by 1-1/4 by 17 in., S-4-S.

2 lower front and back rails, 5/8 by 2-1/2 by 17 in., S-4-S.

1 back rail, 3/4 by 2-1/4 by 17 in., S-4-S.

1 back rail, 3/4 by 2 by 17 in., S-4-S.

1 slat, 3/8 by 3 by 13-1/2 in., S-4-S.

2 slats, 3/8 by 1-1/2 by 13-1/2 in., S-4-S.

Square up the front posts to length. From the single piece specified cut out the back posts, giving them the amount of slant indicated in the drawing. Set these four posts upright in the positions they are to occupy relative to one another in the finished piece, and mark off, as with penciled circles, the approximate locations of mortises. After this, lay them on the bench side by side, even the lower ends and locate accurately the ends of the mortises. Gauge their sides.

Saw the rails to length and lay out the shoulder lines and the cheeks of the tenons and cut them. Plan to house the ends of the slats in the back rails.

While the drawing shows a chair in which the front and back are of equal width, the amateur may make the back narrower if he so desires. A measurement of a common chair will give the proportions.

Place the front and the back in the clamps and after the glue has had time to harden, assemble the remaining parts. Thoroughly scrape and sandpaper all the parts, carefully removing any surplus glue. Wood finish will not "take hold" where any glue has been allowed to remain.

The seat may be given the same treatment as suggested for the armchair. This should not be done, however, until the finish has been applied.

A simple finish is obtained by the application of a coat of paste filler of a soft brown color, if oak has been used. Apply and clean this off in the manner directed by the manufacturers and after it has had 24 hours in which to harden, sand it lightly with No. 00 paper. Over this apply a thin coat of shellac. Allow this to harden, then sandpaper lightly with fine paper. Upon the shellac apply several coats of some good rubbing wax. Follow the directions that are to be found upon the cans, being careful not to apply too much at a time. If too much wax is applied, it stays in the small pores of the wood and produces an ugly chalk-like appearance.

PART VI. ANOTHER PIANO BENCH

ANOTHER PIANO BENCH

The piano bench shown is best made of black walnut or oak and should be finished in the natural color for walnut, but stained some rich brown for oak.

The following pieces will be needed:

1 top, 1 by 15-1/2 by 38-1/2 in., S-2-S.
2 legs, 1 by 14-1/2 by 20-1/2 in., S-4-S.
2 rails, 7/8 by 3-3/4 by 36-1/2 in., S-2-S.
1 stretcher, 3/4 by 4-1/4 by 37 in., S-2-S.

The keys can be secured from the waste that will be cut off from the other parts.

Square up the top in the usual manner to the size indicated in the working drawing. In a similar manner square up the stretcher to width and length.

There will be no need to square the ends of the rails as they are to be cut off on a slant. Square up the sides or edges and then lay off and cut the slanting ends, smoothing them with the plane. Lay off and work the shape on their under edges.

The ends are best laid off by means of a template or pattern for which a piece of rather heavy paper will do. Lay off the main dimensions on a center line. Sketch in the curve of the edge after the slant has been laid out. Lay out the form at the bottom, then fold the paper along the center line and trace the other half. With this pattern lay off the outline upon the wood. For convenience in laying out the grooves for the rails and the mortise for the tenon on the stretcher, it is well to work a face edge upon each leg and allow this to remain until these joints have been made and the parts fitted. The shape at the bottom of the leg is merely suggestive and

45

may be modified as desired.

Lay out and work the tenons on the stretcher. Then lay out and work the grooves upon the rails. Each side of each rail is grooved 1/8 in, to allow the leg to be recessed. This is done to give the bench the bracing that is needed to make it stand firmly. Work the grooves in the legs and the mortises for the rails.

It should be noted that the mortise for the key in the stretcher must be laid out before the shoulders and cheeks of the tenon on which the mortise is made are cut off. Otherwise there would be no place to put the gauge in marking the sides of the mortise for the key.

Thoroughly scrape all the parts and then assemble them. No glue is needed. The rails are held in place by dowel pins, the heads of which are allowed to project slightly and rounded so as to give an ornamental effect. The top is attached by means of small angle irons or by means of blocks and screws fastened to the corners made by top and rails.

ANOTHER SCREEN

The screen shown in the accompanying illustration is made of burlap and plain-sawed oak. The stock list follows:

2 posts, 1-1/2 by 1-1/2 by 40 in., S-4-S.
2 base pieces, 3 by 3 by 12-1/2 in., S-4-S.
2 horizontals, 3/4 by 4-1/4 by 38 in., S-2-S.
1 horizontal, 3/4 by 1-1/2 by 38 in., S-2-S.
1 vertical, 3/4 by 1-3/4 by 20 in., S-2-S.
4 braces, 1-1/8 by 4-1/4 by 6-1/2 in., S-2-S.

The two base pieces may be shaped first. The drawing shows the form and the dimensions. Make use of a face edge in laying out the mortises in the base pieces for the uprights, before these face edges are removed to make the slanting sides.

Work the verticals to length, laying out and cutting the tenons at the bottoms, and shaping the tops as shown.

Lay out and shape the three horizontals as shown, working the tenons upon the ends of each and the mortises in the lower two for the tenons of the middle vertical.

For the braces, secure a face edge on each piece and square one end of each to that. Lay off the curve free-hand upon one block and cut it out. Use this block as a pattern or template to lay off the others.

Thoroughly scrape and sandpaper all the parts, then assemble them, using clamps and good hot glue. Take care to see that there is no warp in the frame as it lies in the clamps. After the glue on the frame has hardened, remove the clamps and attach the base blocks and the braces. The braces are secured by means of round-head screws.

Remove the surplus glue and then apply a finish as desired.

For the paneling, frames will be needed about which to fasten the burlap. These may be made of 1/2-in, soft wood and the following pieces will be necessary:

2 pieces, 1/2 by 2 by 36 in., S-2-S.
2 pieces, 1/2 by 2 by 8 in., S-2-S.
4 pieces, 1/2 by 2 by 18 in., S-2-S.
4 pieces, 1/2 by 2 by 19 in., S-2-S.

Make these frames enough smaller than the openings they are to occupy to allow for burlap and tacks. These frames are held in place by putting fixed nails in the top of each frame before the burlap is attached. Holes are bored in the rails to correspond to them. The lower edges of the frames are held in place by nails inserted up through the rails upon which the frames rest.

A FOLDING CARD TABLE

The accompanying sketch shows the details of a card table that can be folded up and carried about or stored away when not in use. We would advise making two tables at the same time, as the material for both can be purchased nearly as cheaply as for one. The material necessary for making one table is given in the following list:

1 piece, 7/8 by 1-3/16 by 27-1/2 in., basswood or poplar.
2 pieces, 7/8 by 1-3/16 by 29-1/4 in., basswood or poplar.
4 legs, 1 in. square, 24-3/4 in. long; oak.
4 pieces, 1 in. square, 5 in. long; oak.
4 side pieces, 3/8 by 1-3/8 by 29-5/8 in.; oak.
4 pieces, 27-1/2 in. long, single groove electric wire moulding with batten.
1 piece cardboard, 1/8 in. thick, 29-1/4 in. square.
4 pieces brass rod, 3-16 in. diameter, 15 in. long.
30 small copper washers, 3/8 or 7/16 in. outside diameter and drilled 3/16 in.
4 brass corners, 1-3/8 in, deep.
2-1/2 doz. No. 5 oval head brass screws, 3/4 in. long.
4 No. 2, 7/8-in. rubber screw tips.
1 piece felt, 1 yd. square.
1 sheet wadding, 1 yd. square (if pad is wanted under felt).
1 pt. wood stain.
3 doz. No. 14 wire beads, 2 in. long.
Some 2-oz., 4-oz., and 6-oz. flat-head tacks.

Begin by squaring up the four legs making them all 24-3/4 in. long and 1 in. square. Also square up the crosspieces marked B in the detail drawing.

These should be 5 in. long and should have 1/4-in. holes about 1 in. deep drilled in both ends of each for the 1/4-in. oak swivel pins. Measure back 1-1/2 in. from one end of each and bore a 9/16-in. hole, 7/8 in. deep as shown. Now cut a tenon on one end of each leg, 3/4 in. long, that will fit tightly in this 9/16-in. hole. Round the corners of the piece B at the top as shown at C. Fasten the two pieces together with glue and brads, being careful to get them square with each other. After the glue is set bore a 3/16-in. hole in the center of the leg, 7 in. from the edge of the crosspiece, for the brace rod. Bevel the corners as shown. Sandpaper them smooth, then stain and polish.

Lay the two pieces marked D and E in the sketch on a level surface with the 7/8-in. edge up, place the cardboard on top and tack it fast to the pieces, using 6-oz. tacks. Place the center piece in and tack it fast also. Fasten the ends to the other pieces with brads. The four pieces of electric wire moulding should each measure exactly 27-1/2 in. long, or the same length as the center piece. Fit a piece of wood about 4 in. long in the groove at each end of the moulding, plane down and fasten with brads. Next take the thin batten or covering strip that comes with the moulding and bore a 1/2-in. hole in the center, 6 in, from one end, and a 1/4-in. hole, 8-3/16 in. from the other end. With a gouge cut a slot 1/4 in. wide from one hole to the other in the center as shown in the section A-A. Sandpaper this slot smooth and then fasten the batten to the moulding with small brads driven in about 2 in. apart. At a point 3/4 in. from each end and in the center drill 1/4-in. holes through the moulding at the small ends of the slots. These are for the ends of the brace rods to spring into, to lock the legs when they are open. Tack the two pieces of moulding marked F and J on the remaining edges of the cardboard with the slots facing in and the large holes of the slots at opposite sides, then place the other two pieces (G and H) 5 in. inside of these, or just the length of the cross ends of the legs, with the slots facing the first two placed (F and J) and tack fast with 4-oz. tacks. Use brads at the ends and be careful that they do not enter the 1/4-in. holes. This part of the table can now be stained or painted the same as the legs. The 3/8-in. side pieces can also be stained at this time.

The ends of the brass rods can be bent in a vise. One end should be 1 in. long and should be square with the stock. Measure 11-1/4 in. center to center and bend in opposite direction, leaving this end at a slight angle out from square. Just at this bend raise a burr with a sharp chisel to keep the washer on. Now place five of the copper washers on the 1-in. end and batter the end of the rod so they will not slip off. They should be loose so that they will roll and slip on the brace. Slip a washer on the other end and put the end of the rod through the 3/16-in. hole in the leg from the short end side, place another washer on the rod, saw off and rivet down the end.

To put the legs in the table, slip the end of one of the braces and the washers in the large hole in the slot, shove it up until the 1/4-in. hole in the crosspiece and the one in the moulding meet, then drive an oak dowel or rod into each end. This is the hinge or pivot that the legs swing on. When the leg is extended the end of the brace rod should spring into the 1/4-in. hole in the moulding and lock the leg in place. Rubber tips should be put on the bottom ends of the legs. Two wooden buttons should be made and fastened to the cardboard as shown at K for locking the legs when they are closed.

The felt can now be put on the top of the table. Stretch it tightly and then tack the edges securely to the sides of the table. Now fasten on the 3/8-in. side pieces and the brass corners with the small brass screws as shown on the drawing, and the table is complete.

MAGAZINE STAND

If you do not possess the necessary tools for getting out the material used in this piece of furniture, it can be purchased from a mill already planed, sanded and cut to lengths given in the list. Any kind of wood can be used, but quarter-sawed red oak with a mission stain and waxed, gives the best appearance. The following pieces will be needed:

2 shelves, 3/8 by 8 by 15 in., S-2-S.
1 shelf, 3/8 by 10 by 15 in., S-2-S.
1 shelf, 3/8 by 12 by 15 in., S-2-S.
8 slats, 3/8 by 1-1/8 by 38 in., S-4-S.
2 slats, 1/4 by 1-1/8 by 38 in., S-4-S.
4 doz. 1 in. No. 9 round-head screws.

Take the four shelves and line them up with their backs and ends even and clamp them together firmly. Mark the places for the slats across the edges of the shelves, making the first line 1/2 in. from their ends. Use a square to get the lines at right angles to the surface. Another line is drawn 1-1/8 in. from the first, or the width of the slat. The ends of the shelves are marked in the same manner, beginning from the back edges and making the first line 1/2 in. from them, and then another line 1-1/8 in. from the first, or the width of the slat. Make a line across the ends, 1/2 in. from the front edge of the 8-in. shelves, and another line 1-1/8 in. back from the first one. This will leave 2-1/2 in. and 4-1/2 in. of space respectively from the front edges of the 10-in. and 12-in. shelves. Shift the shelves so they will be even on the front edges and mark them the same as the back. Make a 1/4-in. depth mark on all edges between the lines and cut this material out. This can be done while the shelves are clamped together.

Place the shelves on end in their order and start by screwing on the back slats on both ends first, then screw on the two front slats. Turn the stand down and put on the two back slats. Attach the two front slats on the top shelf first. Then bore the places for the remaining holes and turn in the screws. This will bend the slats into place. The two remaining slats are screwed on the ends of the shelves without letting them in, making the spaces equal. Mark each slat 1/2 in. below the bottom shelf and saw them off. The stand can be taken apart, sandpapered and stained.

A TABOURET

The stock necessary to make a tabouret of craftsman design as shown in the accompanying illustration can be purchased from the mill ready cut to length, squared and sanded. Quarter-sawed oak is the best wood to use and it is also the easiest to secure. Order the following pieces:

4 legs, 1-1/2 in. square by 22 in. long.
1 top, 3/4 in. thick by 14 in. square.
4 top rails, 3/4 by 4 by 12 in.
4 lower rails, 3/4 by 3 by 12 in.

First square up the four legs. Bevel the tops at an angle of 30 deg. and hollow out the lower part of the legs as shown in the detail sketch. Clamp them together with the ends square and lay out the mortises all at once. Cut the tenons on the rails to fit these mortises. Lay them out in the same manner as the posts so as to get them all the same distance between shoulders. The upper rails should be cut out underneath as shown.

The rails and posts can now be glued together. Be careful to get them joined perfectly square. When they are dry cut and fit the top as shown. This is fastened to the top rails by means of screws from the inside. Remove all surplus glue from about the joints, as the finish will not take where there is any glue. Go over the whole with fine sandpaper and remove all rough spots, then apply the finish you like best.

A PORCH SWING

The porch swing shown in the illustration can be made of southern pine at a very moderate cost. It should be suspended by rustless black chains and eyebolts passing through the lower rails. If cushions are desired they can be made up quite cheaply of elastic felt covered with denim cloth.

These pieces, dressed and sanded, may be bought at the mill:

2 rails, 1-3/4 by 3 by 71 in., S-4-S.
1 rail, 1-3/4 by 3 by 65 in., S-4-S.
2 posts, 1-3/4 by 3 by 25 in., S-4-S.
2 posts, 1-3/4 by 3 by 17 in., S-4-S.
2 rails, 1-3/4 by 3 by 22-1/2 in., S-2-S.
2 arm rests, 7/8 by 4 by 28 in., S-2-S.
5 slats, 3/8 by 5 by 16 in., S-2-S.

8 ft. flooring for bottom.

2 cleats, 7/8 by 1-1/2 by 57 in., S-4-S.

Plane and square the ends of all the rails and posts. Lay out the lap joints for the back rails and posts. Use a knife line for this and saw exactly to the line to avoid trimming with the chisel. When sawing be careful to cut exactly halfway through the thickness of each piece. In the same way make the lap joints between the front rail and posts. Have the two end rails exactly the same length and proceed to fasten the front and back posts to them, using 4-in. lag screws and washers. Bore through the posts and part way into the ends of the end rails for the lag screws.

The slats are mortised 1/2 in. into the back rails, or a 3/8-in. groove may be planed in these rails, the entire distance between joints, to receive the slats. A rabbeting plane will be needed for this. The arm rests lap over the back posts and are held to them with 2-in. round-head screws. They may be fastened to the top of the front posts with round-head screws or dowel pins.

Ordinary pine flooring makes a good, tight seat, or 7/8-in. board may be used if desired. Fasten the cleats, which support the seat, to the front and back lower rails with 1-1/2-in. screws.

To bring out the beautiful grain of southern pine, stain it brown or black and finish with two coats of waterproof varnish.

PART VII. A FOOT WARMER

A FOOT WARMER

This foot warmer is so constructed that two bricks may be heated and placed inside of the stool.

Oak is the most suitable wood to use, and the following pieces will be needed:

4 legs, 1-1/4 by 1-1/4 by 8 in., S-4-S.

4 side rails, 7/8 by 3 by 8-1/2 in., S-2-S.

4 top pieces, 7/8 by 1-1/2 by 12 in., S-2-S.

1 bottom piece, 7/8 by 8-1/2 by 8-1/2 in., S-2-S.

1 piece asbestos, 8-1/2 by 8-1/2 in.

4 pieces asbestos, 2 by 8-1/2 in.

1 sheet of brass, 13 by 13 in., 17 gauge.

2 hinges, 1 elbow catch, 3 doz. ornamental tacks.

The work may be started by shaping the four legs and cutting the mortises for the rails. Tenons are cut on the ends of the rails to fit in the mortises made in the posts. They are then glued together, care being taken to get the stool perfectly square.

The top frame can now be made and covered with the sheet of brass. The frame has mitered corners and the inside of the frame must be even with the inside of the rails. This in turn is fastened to the stool with the two hinges on the back and the elbow catch on the front side to keep it closed.

The design on the brass can be made by tacking it on a board, laying out the design and piercing the background with some sharp-pointed tool. This leaves the design raised with a smooth surface.

The brass can now be removed from the board, placed on the frame and fastened with the ornamental tacks.

Turn the stool bottom side up and line the inside of the rails with asbestos; then place the bricks on the inside of the stool. Both should fit up tight to the brass when the bottom is in place.

The stool is now ready for the finish, which can be of some stain to match the other furniture in the room where it is to be used.

A PLATE RACK FOR THE DINING ROOM

This plate rack can be made of any kind of wood and finished to match other pieces of furniture in the room, but as it is of mission design, oak is the most suitable lumber, as it takes the mission stain so nicely.

The material required is as follows:

4 posts, 1-1/2 by 1-1/2 by 28 in., S-4-S.
1 top, 7/8 by 7-1/4 by 48 in., S-2-S.
2 plate rails, 7/8 by 6-1/4 by 32 in., S-2-S.
2 back boards, 7/8 by 7-1/4 by 25 in., S-2-S.
2 side boards, 7/8 by 5-1/4 by 25 in., S-2-S.
4 shelves, 7/8 by 6-1/2 by 8-1/4 in., S-2-S.
2 plate rests, 7/8 by 7/8 by 32 in., S-4-S.

This stock is specified to exact thickness, but some allowance is made for trimming on the edges and ends.

Begin work by squaring up the posts to length and beveling the top ends, then trim the back and side boards. These are nailed together, lapping the back board over the side board. The posts are fastened with dowels placed at equal distances apart. Hot glue is used in the joints.

The four shelves are now put in place. These are notched out to fit around the posts and are nailed and glued.

While the glue is hardening on these, the plate rails can be cut. These have 7/8-in grooves near the front edge to receive the lower edge of the plates when resting against the two strips placed 5 in. above the plate rails and far enough back to prevent the plates from falling forward.

The rails are fastened to the two sides with dowels, three at each end being sufficient. The two strips fit in mortises cut in the side pieces. The top is then put on. This fits around the posts and rests on the sides. Hooks on which to hang cups are placed under the rails. All parts are thoroughly sandpapered before the stain is applied.

A MISSION SIDEBOARD

The sideboard is a piece designed to go with the armchair and side chair with similar paneling design. Like these chairs the sideboard should be made of hard wood and should be similarly finished. The drawer pulls, if not made of wood, should be of such metal and design as to harmonize with the mission style. Wrought-iron effects in plain outlines are appropriate.

Drawer sides, bottoms and backs may be made of some soft wood, such as yellow poplar. The small top drawer may be lined with ooze leather for holding silverware.

Obtain the following stock:

2 posts, 2 by 2 by 50 in., S-4-S.
2 posts, 2 by 2 by 39 in., S-4-S.
1 top, 1 by 23 by 58 in., S-2-S.
2 plate rails, 1/2 by 2 by 58 in., S-4-S.
1 plate rail, 1/2 by 1-1/2 by 58 in., S-4-S.
2 rails, 7/8 by 2 by 21 in., S-4-S.
2 rails, 7/8 by 2-1/2 by 21 in., S-4-S.
2 rails, 7/8 by 3 by 21 in., S-4-S.
4 slats, 3/8 by 1-1/2 by 10-1/2 in., S-4-S.
2 slats, 3/8 by 3-1/2 by 10-1/2 in., S-4-S.
2 panels, 3/8 by 18-3/4 by 10 in., S-2-S.
1 back rail, 7/8 by 2 by 54 in., S-4-S.
1 back rail, 7/8 by 3-1/8 by 54 in., S-4-S.
1 back rail, 7/8 by 3 by 54 in., S-4-S.
2 back stiles, 7/8 by 1-3/4 by 11 in., S-4-S.
2 back stiles, 7/8 by 2-1/2 by 11 in., S-4-S.
1 back panel, 3/8 by 10 by 24-1/2 in., S-2-S.
1 back panel, 3/8 by 11-1/2 by 53 in., S-2-S.
2 back panels, 3/8 by 11 by 11 in., S-2-S.
1 drawer front, 3/4 by 3 by 24-1/2 in., S-4-S.
2 drawer fronts, 3/4 by 4 by 24-1/2 in., S-4-S.
2 drawer fronts, 3/4 by 6 by 52-1/2 in., S-4-S.
2 drawer ends, 1/2 by 3 by 20 in., S-4-S, poplar.
4 drawer ends, 1/2 by 4 by 20 in., S-4-S, poplar.
4 drawer ends, 5/8 by 6 by 20 in., S-4-S, poplar.
3 drawer backs, 3/8 by 4 by 24 in., S-2-S, poplar.
2 drawer backs, 3/8 by 6 by 52 in., S-2-S, poplar.
3 drawer bottoms, 3/8 by 20 by 24 in., S-2-S, poplar.
2 drawer bottoms, 3/8 by 20 by 52 in., S-2-S, poplar.
2 drawer supports, 3/4 by 2-1/2 by 24-1/2 in., S-4-S.
4 drawer supports, 3/4 by 2-1/2 by 54 in., S-4-S.
10 drawer slides, 3/4 by 2 by 22 in., S-4-S.
2 middle verticals, 3/4 by 22 by 13 in., S-2-S.

Drawer guides can be made from scrap stock.

A detailed description is hardly necessary for such a piece of work as this. Anyone capable of building it, will know the order of the different operations that are required in its construction.

It may be said that the two back panels at either side of the small drawers may be filled with beveled plate glass instead of wood if one so choose.